DOORWAYS, WINDOWS & TRANSOMS
Stained Glass Pattern Book

ANNA CROYLE

DOVER PUBLICATIONS, INC.
MINEOLA, NEW YORK

Laco

Bibliographical Note

Doorways, Windows & Transoms Stained Glass Pattern Book is a new work, first published by Dover Publications, Inc., in 2008.

DOVER *Pictorial Archive* SERIES

International Standard Book Number
ISBN-13: 978-0-486-46235-6
ISBN-10: 0-486-46235-8

Manufactured in the United States by LSC Communications
46235810   2018
www.doverpublications.com

PUBLISHER'S NOTE

Based on remains found at Pompeii, stained glass was used by wealthy Romans in their villas and palaces in the first century AD. The use of stained glass in the home thrives today. The areas around doorways are favored for the installation of stained glass windows — to the sides of the door (sidelights), above the door (fanlights and transoms), and on the door itself (rectangles, ovals, and circles). This volume contains over 90 graceful stained glass patterns. Just a few of the motifs include irises, roses, tulips, morning glories, daffodils, grapes, and pineapples. There are many striking abstract patterns as well. You can reproduce these patterns in smaller or larger sizes.

All materials needed, including general instructions and tools for beginners, can be purchased from local craft and hobby stores, or on the Internet.

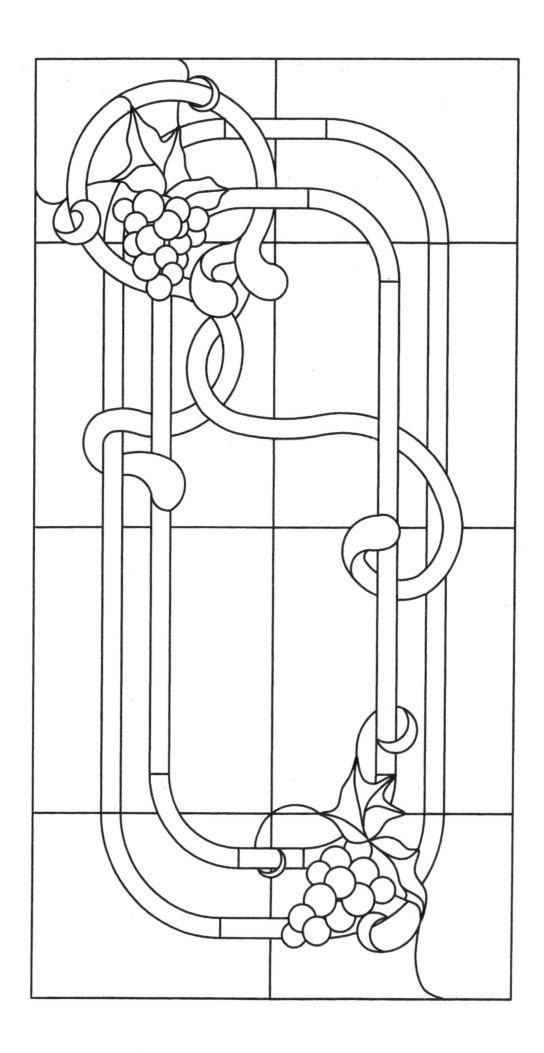

4

7

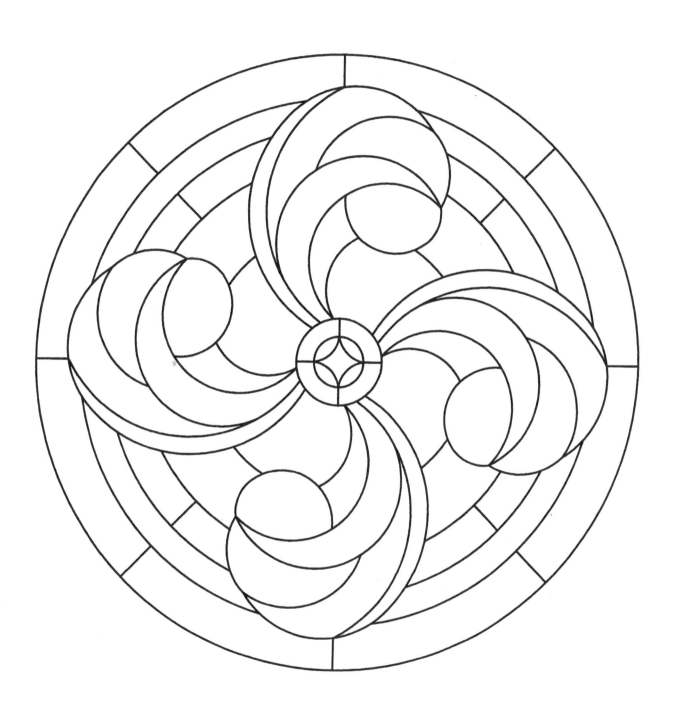

14

17

19

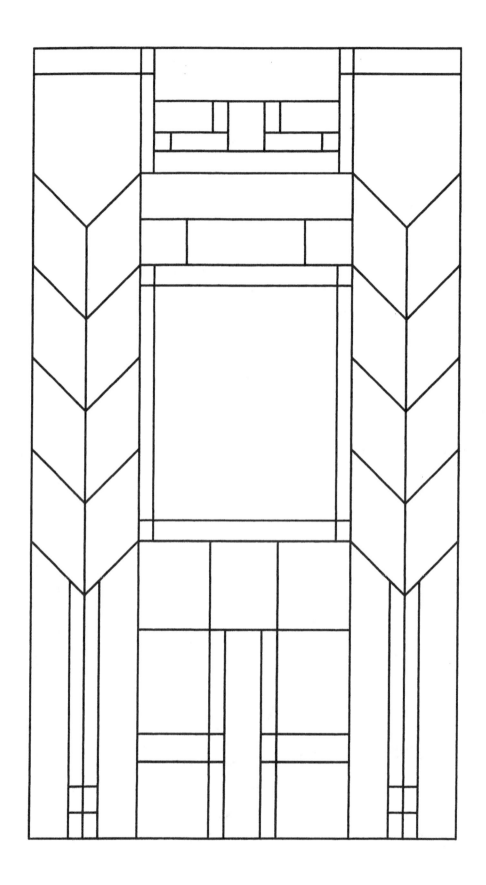

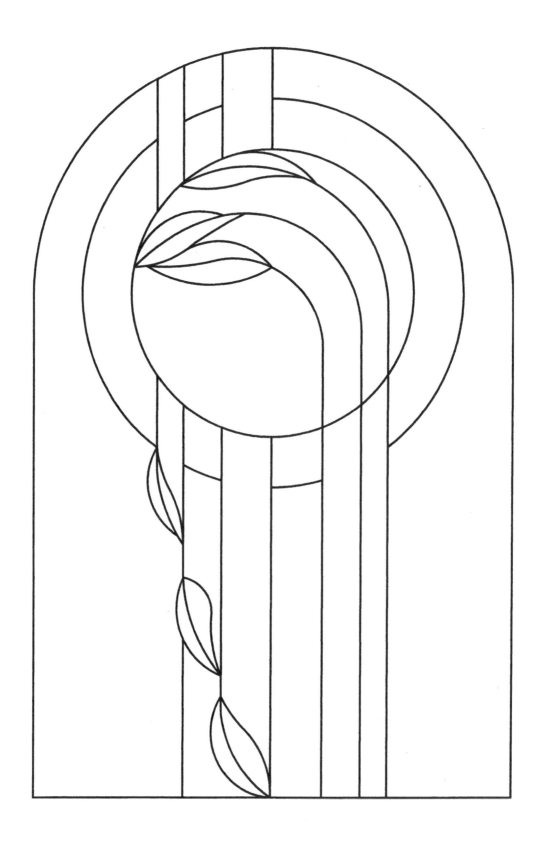

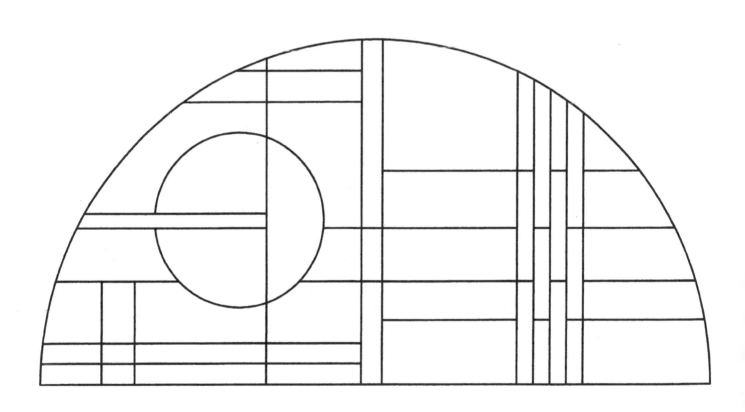

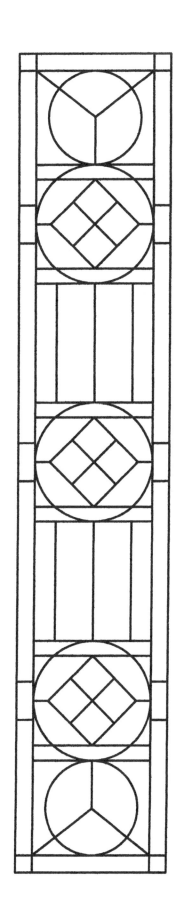

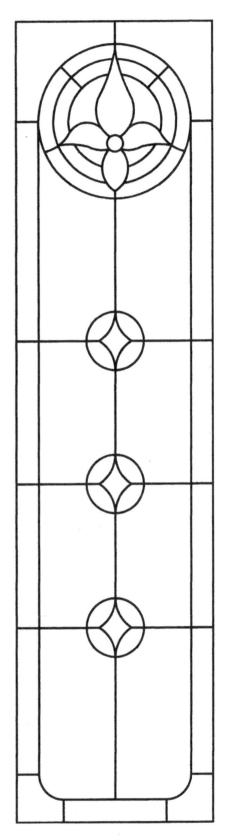

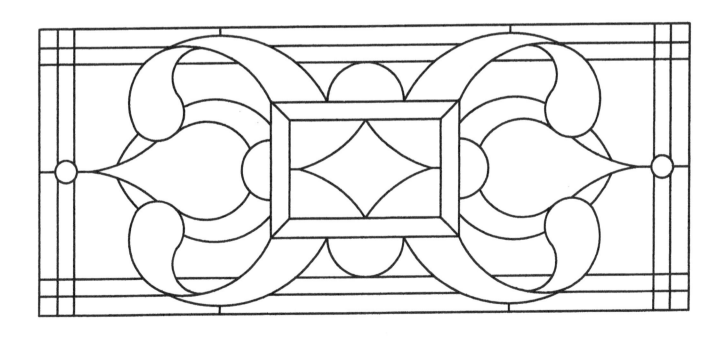

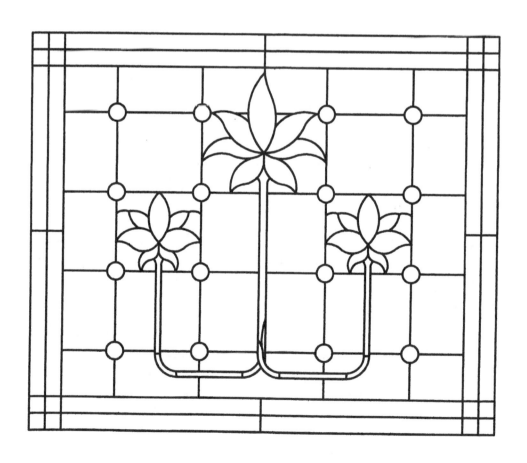

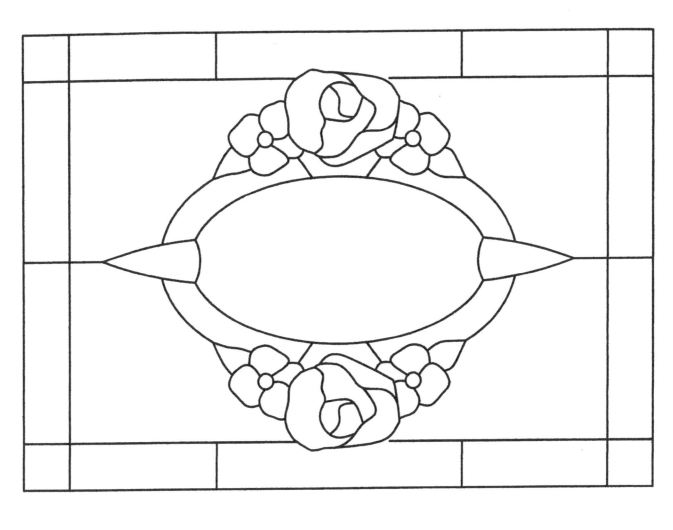

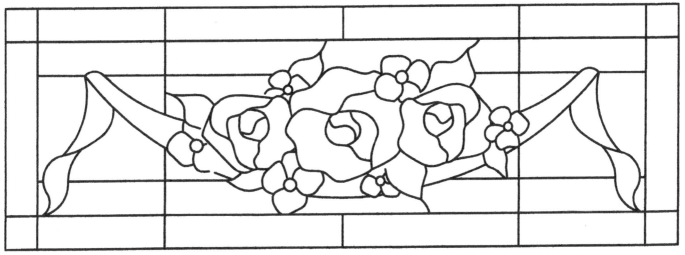

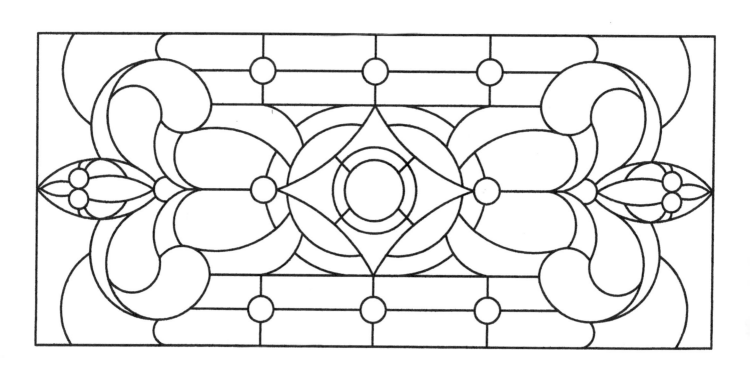

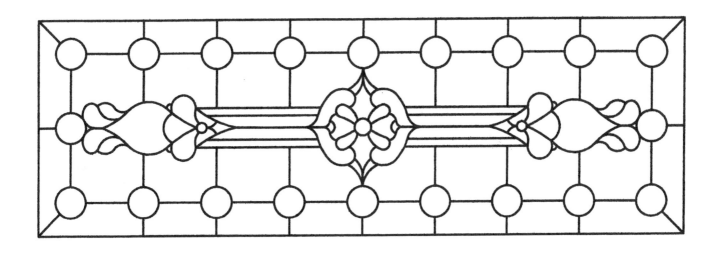

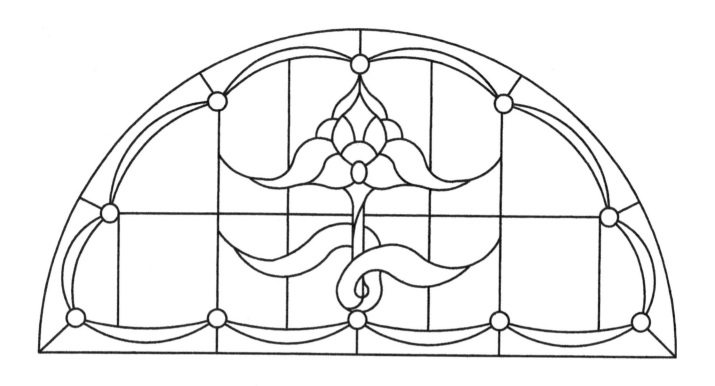

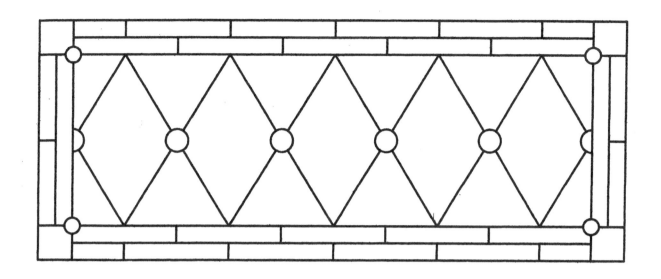

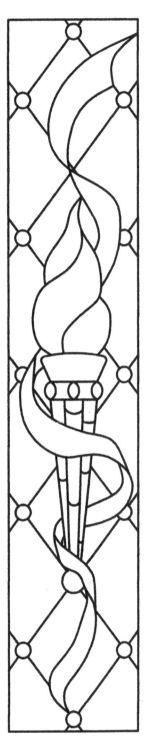

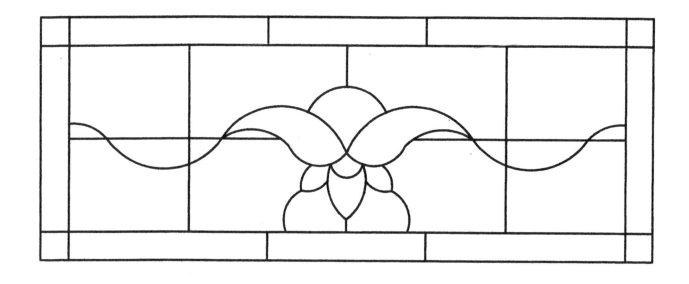

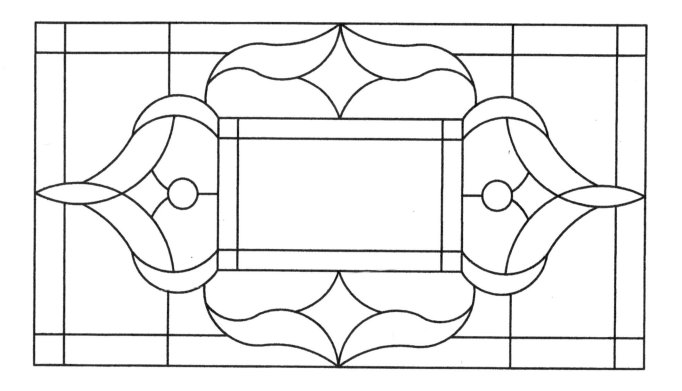

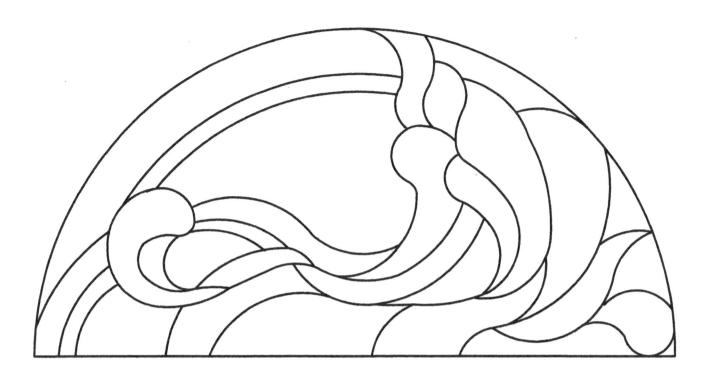

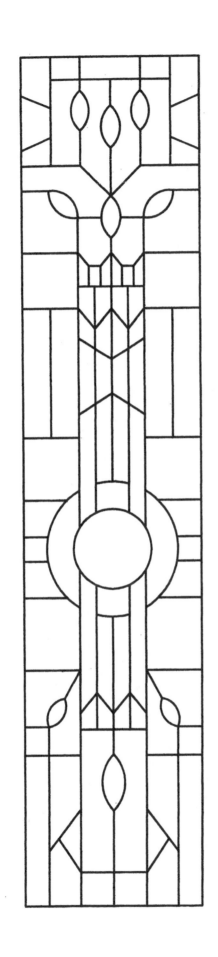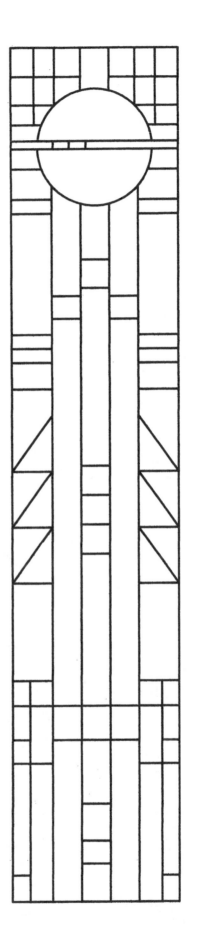

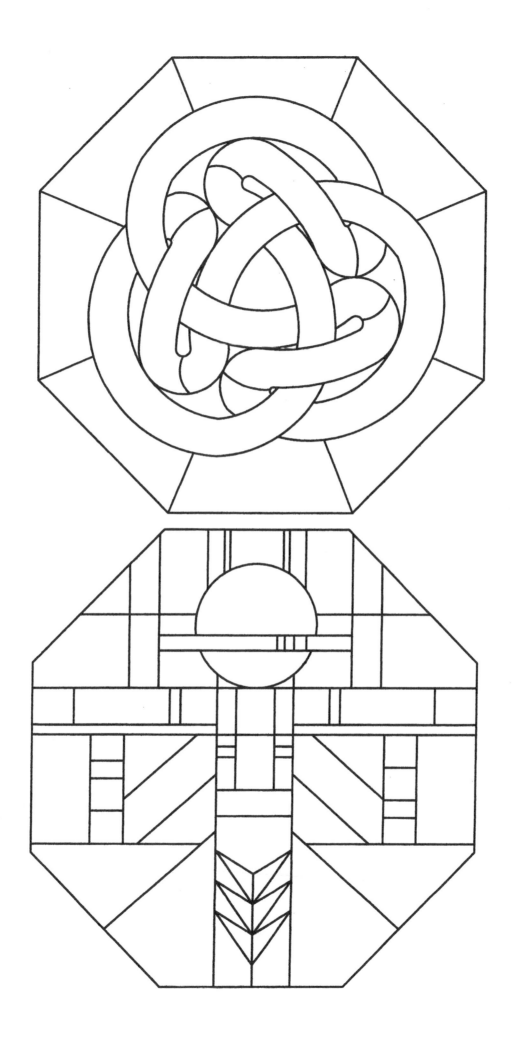

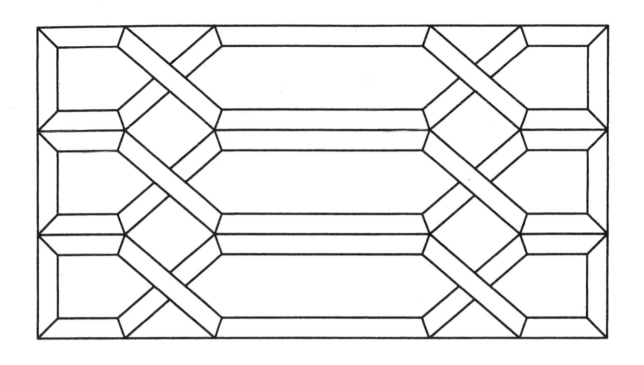

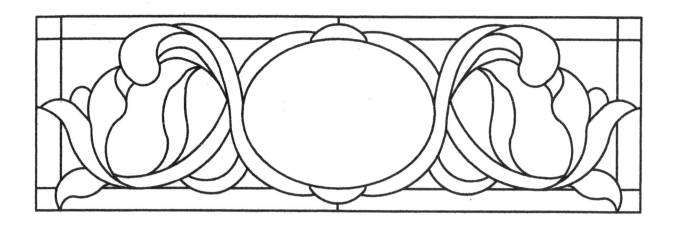

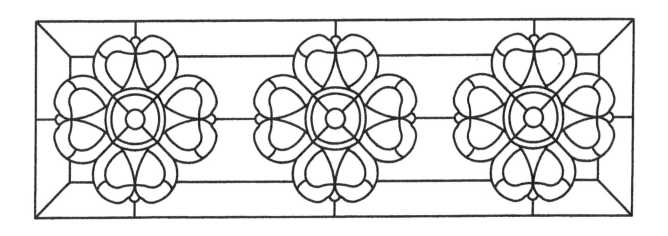

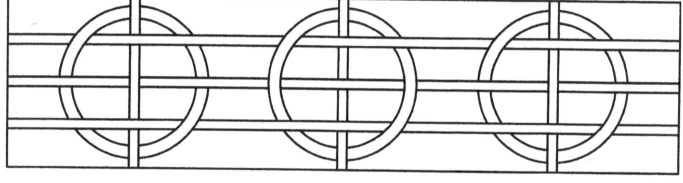

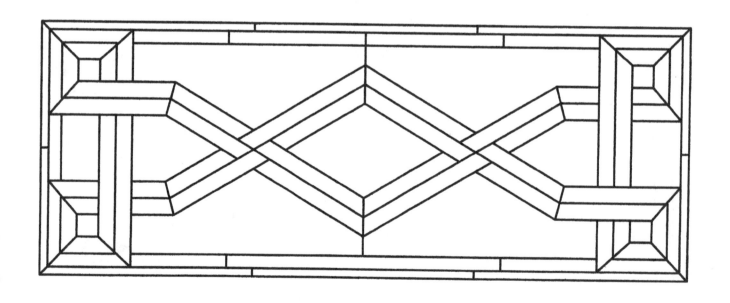

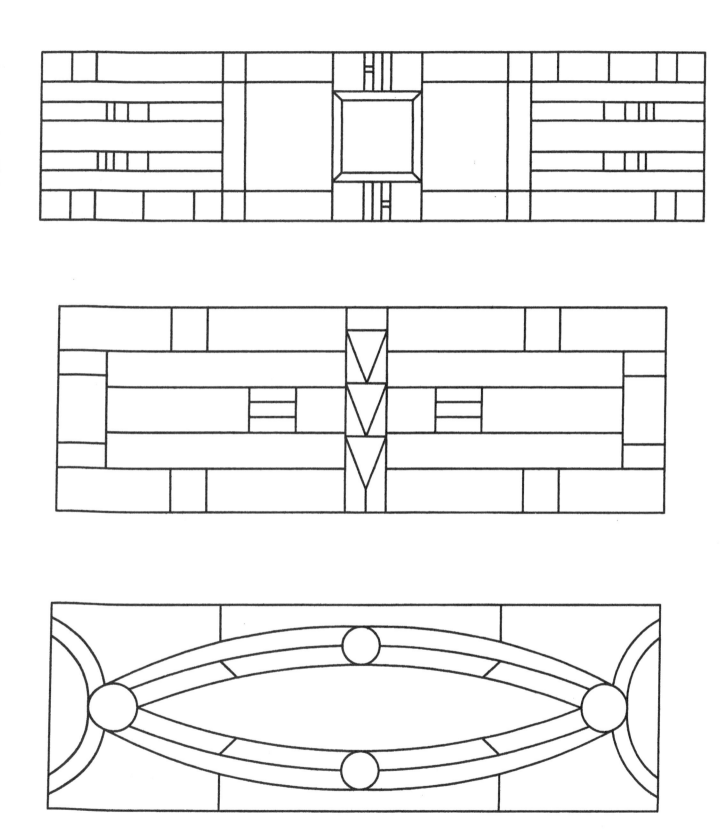